# GOD MADE
# MILLIONAIRE ®

You're One Instruction Away From Your
God-Given Dream Becoming A Reality!

## TC Bradley

# GOD MADE
# MILLIONAIRE ®

You're One Instruction Away From Your
God-Given Dream Becoming A Reality!

## TC Bradley

# DEDICATION

First and foremost, I would like to dedicate this book to my beautiful wife of 28 plus years, Vickie Bradley.

You are truly the wind beneath my wings.

I LOVE you, Sweetheart…Peas and Carrots Forever.

I would also like to dedicate this book to my two AWESOME twin grandsons, Dionis and Jayden Mejia and my beautiful granddaughter, Lexi Owens.

Your "Grandpa Genius" loves you with all of his heart.

I would also like to dedicate this book to a GREAT man of God who passed away last year, who had a POWERFUL impact on my life with his ministry, Dr. Norval Hayes.

To my Legacy family and Damon Davis, thank you for helping take my message to the Nations…I LOVE being part of your family.

Finally, I would like to acknowledge the GREATEST business partner I could ever hope or dream or wish for… Jesus Christ.

# CONTENTS

# FORWARD

TC Bradley and I opened our Media and Publishing agencies at the same time. A fellow veteran, we immediately connected not as competitors but as colleagues, supernatural brothers that had a fiber optic that ran through both of us. And that fiber optic was Supernatural. I am not a stranger of this, because I had experienced it my entire life.

Three days before the Christmas of 2017, I had a vision of doing an event in New York Times Square of experts speaking at NASDAQ. I wasn't clear on who was going to speak. Over time, it became clear that it would be CEO's in the niche. About the same time, TC published his book "Supernatural Success".

I knew no one in this niche. Before TC released his book, I got an advance digital version to review. I immediately read through it. He also released a promotional video about the book as well that contained testimonials of others who had experienced Supernatural Success.

Supernatural Success leads you to people that can help you reach your goals. After watching the video, I had a unique feeling that I had never felt before. My heart rate increased while watching the video. I was deeply touched and inspired by the message.

I found an article written by a colleague in our circle that was related to the topic of the niche I was targeting. He was literally in my mastermind group and I had never seen him post anything or make a comment in the group.

Once I saw the name of the person that wrote the article, I went back to check if he was a member of our group and he was. I immediately reached out to make an appointment and share the vision of the event I had with him. We came to an agreement to hold the event and he promised to introduce me to clients in the niche that would be interested in attending the event.

I created a "Win-Win" situation. He didn't like doing the logistics of an event, but I did. It was a good match.

In TC's book, Supernatural Success he mentions, "Life can change for you in a moment."

I began to implement what TC was saying in his book. I am not a stranger to this because I have had several Supernatural Success in my life because I know I am blessed and highly favored. But it's important to stay consistent in practice.

From conception to reality in a period of less than 90 days, resulted in one of the biggest events in the space, held in Times Square New York where CEO's came in from around the world.

End Result, a high six-figure revenue. I never doubted that I could pull it off with the help of Supernatural Success.

If you have not read all of TC's books, I highly recommend it. I often refer to his book "Supernatural Success" to sharpen my saw. TC is the quintessential leader and mentor. And I am very grateful and appreciative for our relationship.

May you be blessed and highly favored and may you realize Supernatural Success and Prosperity!

T. Allen Hanes

www.TAllenHanes.com

# INTRODUCTION

I want to start this book by first saying Thank You for your investment in this book. I recognize that the marketplace is flooded with books, and you could easily purchase any other book, but you trusted me and choose this one. I want you to know that I don't take that trust lightly, and will do my very best to overdeliver and make an impact in your life and your business if you apply these principles.

It is important to me that you know upfront that I have written this book to have a maximum impact in your life.

You should be able to actually read this book in one sitting and re-read it many times.

The chapters are short and concise by design.

One of the biggest and most frequent compliments I received after writing my last book, *"Supernatural Success: Spiritual Laws I Used To Generate Over A Million Dollars In Sales And Beat Oprah In Website Traffic"* was the fact that people not only read the book once but several times.

Oh, and there is the businessman who added 300k CASH money into his business account within 45 days of reading that book, and the businesswoman who only read the first 3 chapters and deposited 10k CASH into her account...so there's that! ☺

My goal for you is to have several "AHA" moments while reading this book.

Literally, moments where the clouds part and you "know that you know" that you were given an instruction or received the inspiration that will activate that God-given dream that is placed inside of you.

Just reading the first chapter can transform your world and that change can be <u>instantaneous</u>.

What this book is NOT is a bunch of scriptures or an attempt to convert you over to a certain theology.

Those that want to argue theology with me can save their time right now.

I have no interest in engaging in such time-wasting activities.

I am too busy running my successful businesses to be concerned with you or your opinions and I make no apologies for that success.

Besides that, a man with a testimony beats a man with a theory any day of the week.

Plus, I come at this topic from a successful businessman's point of view, not a Pastor's point of view.

I built a company to 1.6 million dollars in sales within the first 6 months of business, generating 100k to 150k daily in sales, only to lose that business to a bad partnership.

This was easily a 10 million dollar company and I lost it.

Few businessmen will ever recover from such a <u>devastating</u> event, yet, 1-2 years after this event, I launched my first website which sold over a million dollars globally, and within 2 years' time, I had more website traffic going to that website than Oprah had going to her website.

Within 45 days of publishing Supernatural Success: Spiritual Laws I Used To Generate Over A Million Dollars In Sales And Beat Oprah In Website Traffic" I signed a major TV deal and was featured on five (5) TV networks, including The Word Network, which is seen in 200 nations.

My publishing and media business works has worked with some of the elite entrepreneurs in the world to publish their books, often debuting as a best seller on Amazon, and we recently signed a contract to have our franchise TV segment, "Business Leaders Spotlight" air on a nationally syndicated talk show that is seen in 140 TV markets, including the TOP 3 TV markets, NY, LA and Chicago.

We had only been doing our TV segments for 2 years when we signed this major TV deal that now allows us to feature our clients on national TV.

So when I tell you I am not interested in arguing or defending my point of view expressed in this book with the Pharisees or the religious folks out here, I am not kidding and I am well qualified to talk about this topic.

Keep stepping Sweet Pea as I was not sent to you anyway and this book is not for you.

I was sent to the one that has the God-Given dream that they have kept hidden until now.

I am not sure of what lead you here to get this book, but I can comfortably say that it was not by accident.

I believe that you are here by divine appointment.

I believe that God is up to something BIG in your life, really BIG or you would not be reading these words.

I think you have been playing small long enough and God is saying that NOW is the time for you to rise up and walk in your God-Given purpose.

I believe God Made Millionaires ® will be created because of the lessons and inspiration found in this book.

There's a generation of millionaires, of God Made Millionaires that God is going to raise up.

Will you be one of them?

It's time for YOU to dream again.

It's time for YOU to dream BIG again!

Why Not YOU?

Why Not NOW?

If Not NOW...then When?

*TC Bradley*

# CHAPTER 1

## GOD NEVER CALLED ANYONE TO TAKE A VOW OF POVERTY

Let's get this out in the open right now at the start of this book.

God never called anyone to take a vow of poverty and you are not more self-righteous by being poor than rich.

Being broke doesn't make you holier than me.

This may come as a surprise to some reading this but it's true.

As a matter of fact, some of the early Christians were some of the most prosperous people to walk the earth.

It was hundreds of years later, for political reasons, that this pagan idea that there was virtue in being broke was introduced and again was used in the middle ages to enslave people and keep them down.

This false belief that states somehow, that the more broke you are, the more virtue you have, this has been passed down from generation to generation.

When talking about this topic, people say the goofiest things to defend their beliefs and really sometimes, to justify why they are broke.

**Well, "money can't buy you happiness," they say... well, I say poverty can't buy you anything.**

They will say with great pride, the bible says "The LOVE of money is the root of all evil", 1 Timothy 6:10

Yet the Bible also says, *"but money answereth all things" Ecclesiastes 10:19*

Here is what I want to challenge you to think about if you are hung up about money.

Why would God promise to bless us with something that was evil?

Why would the bible clearly say "All Wealth Comes From the Lord" Deut 8:18, if it were evil?

I have resolved this issue in my mind but you need to resolve it in your mind BEFORE you move on from this chapter.

If you are ever going to walk in the wealth and prosperity that God has for you, this false belief must be forever settled in your mind.

The LOVE of money may be the root of all evil but the LACK of money causes far more damage today.

More people are killed today from lack of money rather than LOVE of money.

More marriages end in divorce today, not because of the LOVE of money but the LACK of money.

Most health-related deaths today are due to lack of money to pay for health care rather than LOVE of money.

Everyday my newsfeed on Facebook is filled with Go Fund Me requests from good people that have a serious need that requires finances. They are not posting this Go Fund Me campaigns because of their LOVE for money but because of a lack of money to take care of an issue in their life.

When I see this heartbreaking "Go Fund Me" campaigns, I am not thinking of "The LOVE of money is the root of all evil" 1 Timothy 6:10

Since I am already neck-deep in this conversation, let's take it to another level.

Most people that are not in church criticize the church for "only being interested in people's money"

Every week in a church somewhere, there are members of that church and even non-members of that church contacting the church for money.

Money to pay a light bill before it is disconnected or a gas bill before it is cut off.

Or money for car payment before it is repossessed.

Or money to pay for groceries for a family that cannot eat unless money is provided.

Every single week, this is a common occurrence in churches all across the United States.

Yet, you want me to believe that the church is all about money and you criticize them when they take an offering up?

Come Monday morning, their phones are going to start ringing with heartfelt requests for money.

The harsh reality is that it takes finances to operate a church today and a LOT of them.

The very BEST thing you can do right now is to make up your mind on this issue and start walking in your God-given purpose, so you can be a Blessing to others.

Better yet, become a God Made Millionaire ®, so you can really help others.

There is no greater feeling in the world than being in a position to help others financially.

I have been on the receiving end and I have been on the giving end.

Trust me; the giving end is a much better place to be.

Settle this issue once and for all and don't let anyone try to convince you that it is your destiny to be broke or poor for the rest of your life.

God has not called you to be broke.

Got it?

Good!

# CHAPTER 2

## THE ELEVATOR TO THE PENTHOUSE

I am about to share a lesson with you that had a PROFOUND and immediate impact on my publishing and media business.

As a matter of fact, the first month that I applied it, our MONTHLY revenue tripled that month.

That was not a small number either.

I always like to teach and speak from experience.

I firmly believe that I could have published this book with only this chapter and if you only applied the teaching in this one chapter, your life and bank accounts could be immediately transformed.

In my case, the first 30 days.

Do I have your attention yet?

Good.

Let's roll.

One of my wife's favorite things to do is to watch the 4th of

July fireworks.

The challenge that we have is that we both really do not like the big crowds that one has to endure to view those fireworks.

This year, I rented a penthouse suite at the Westin in Cape Coral.

We were on the 18th floor, which is the TOP floor on that hotel property, and we had views of several fireworks shows, Cape Coral, Fort Myers and Sanibel Island from the HUGE outside deck.

Now to access the penthouse suite that I had rented for the night, we have to take an elevator to the penthouse.

Now here is the life-changing lesson.

To access the penthouse, we had to enter the elevator and press a button for the 18th floor.

Otherwise, we would simply have to wait in that elevator until someone came in and pushed a button and hope that they would press the 18th-floor button, otherwise we would only rise to the floor that someone else had selected.

This is a POWERFUL parable on how life is.

Most people get on the elevator called life every day and they wait for someone to come in and push a button, they are subject to the whims of whoever enters the elevator and pushes a button and go wherever that person wants to go.

Sometimes, they might even get lucky and someone pushes

the 18th Penthouse suite button, but most of the time, they just ride the elevator of life and only get a glimpse of the Penthouse suite and mostly see the lower tier floors.

Nothing in life happens until you manually push the button of the floor that you want to proceed to.

Nothing.

"Hoping" you are going to go to the penthouse "one day" isn't going to get you there.

"Praying" that you are going to get to go to the penthouse one day, isn't going to get you there.

Asking God to pick a floor that he wants you to be at, "if it be his will" isn't going to get you to the penthouse!

God is NOT going to pick the floor you go on, the car you drive or the home you live in!

God does not care if you live in an apartment or a million-dollar mansion.

Let's get this straight; God is NOT going to choose for you!

Yet, most people do all of the above.

Every. Single. Day.

"If it be your will" they pray.

God's will is pretty simple to understand and figure out, it doesn't take a Greek scholar to understand what the bible meant when it said *"Beloved, I wish above all things that thou mayest prosper and be in health, even as thy soul prospereth" 3 John 2-5*

Listen up...It's Gods will that you push the button on the floor that YOU want.

You pick the floor you want, you select the car you want, and the home you want.

According to <u>your faith,</u> let it be so.

Before I share with you exactly how you can push that button, I want to share another story with you.

45 days after I published my last book, "Supernatural Success" Spiritual Laws I Used To Generate Over a Million Dollars in Website Traffic And Beat Oprah In Website Traffic", I signed a major TV deal based on the book that aired on 5 TV Networks including the WORD Network which is seen in over 200 Nations.

Now, I will discuss in another chapter in detail how I almost didn't publish that book but for this chapter, I have a very valuable lesson for you.

It knocked me back and took the wind out of my chest but it also changed my life and my business.

I was sitting in my office reflecting on how good God has been to me specifically thinking about the Supernatural Success book and the TV deal that came so quickly after I published the book and I started thanking the Lord for opening that door for me for that TV deal to happen.

When I heard the Lord speak to my inner spirit and correct me and say "I didn't open that door for you".

So now, I start an argument with the Lord right there in my office.

"You must certainly did open that door for me, it wasn't me that opened that door Lord, for me to appear on those 5 TV networks, that was all YOU Lord"

"No, it wasn't, I had NOTHING to do with getting you on those TV networks Son" was the response.

"Ok then Lord, then if it wasn't you that opened that door who did?" was my immediate response.

"Simple my Son, It was YOUR FAITH that opened that door to that major TV deal"

"My faith?" I protested.

"Yes, your faith" was the stern response.

Ok Lord, I will play along with you on this, how in the world did my faith open that door for the TV network deal?"

"You wrote the book" was the simple response.

"You almost didn't publish that book but by faith, you did write the book, had you not written and published the book, no TV deal would have ever happened for you"

**"YOUR FAITH opened up that door for you Son, not me."**
**was the final response.**

I sat in stunned silence.

I had always prayed "God, go before me and open doors that need to be open and close the doors in my life that need to be closed" but God doesn't open doors for us or close doors for us or pick the penthouse floor for us.

Our faith does.

My life has NEVER been the same after I was taken to the woodshed in my office that morning by the Lord.

I laugh at how silly it must seem to the Lord that I thought I could win an argument with him.

I am sure I really crack him up sometimes with my shenanigans.

But when I "get it"

I "Got it"

And I don't have to be told twice.

This simple yet profound revelation has been a total game-changer in my business and life.

So how do we push the button and head to the penthouse floor?

There are several things you can do to 'push that button" but I will give you the simplest most POWERFUL way to push that button to the penthouse suite.

"Thou shalt DECREE a thing and it shall come to pass" Job

22:28

Not think about a thing.

Not pray about a thing.

Thou shalt DECREE a thing.

Every day that you don't DECREE what you want in your life, you are standing on that elevator like a Piker, waiting for someone else to pick the floor that you want to go to.

Every.

Single.

Day.

There is not a day that goes by now that I am not DECREE-ING Success and Prosperity on my business.

I call my business's successful.

I speak to my checkbooks and call in millions of dollars into them. (broke people call in hundreds of dollars or nothing at all)

I call clients into my business.

I speak of supernatural opportunities and divine connections that come my way.

I call every bill paid in full.

I call my mortgage paid in full.

Every day that you don't DECREE what you want to be established in your life is another day that someone else is picking

YOUR destination and choosing your DESTINY!

You can choose to apply this one lesson and change your life right now, or you can make the choice to use your FAITH to open some major doors in your life that NO man can close.

Or you can say to yourself, "this is too simple to work and speaking to my checkbook? Whoever heard of such a foolish thing?"

"But God hath chosen the foolish things of the world to confound the wise;" 1 Corinthians 1:27

Keep being wise and broke Sweet Pea or you can choose to use these spiritual laws that work with 100% certainty.

Choose wisely grasshopper.

# CHAPTER 3

## YOU'RE ALREADY A GOD MADE MILLIONAIRE...YOU JUST DON'T KNOW IT YET!

My wife and I actually own 2 federal trademarks on the term "God Made Millionaire"

We actually have a POWERFUL t-shirt line with that term on the shirts.

For me, the shirt is a POWERFUL decree that I am making whenever I wear the shirt, and since we have several designs, I wear them quite a bit.

For me, the term has NEVER been about a bank account but a FAITH account.

One of the first things I did after we secured the trademark rights to the term "God Made Millionaire" was to contact one of the largest faith-based t-shirt companies in the world to negotiate a licensing deal to place the shirts nationwide.

It took some persistence, but I was able to finally get an email response from the CEO and Founder of the company that I wasn't expecting.

"I really don't understand the concept...I mean how many Christian Millionaires are out there and how many of them are going to want to wear a God Made Millionaire Shirt?"

*Completely and totally missing the whole point of the shirt...lol.*

My response?

"Every Christian is a God Made Millionaire...they just don't realize it...yet."

He passed on the license deal and ended up lighting my fuse even more which placed me in a position to prove him wrong.

I have to tell you something that you need to understand when it comes to your God-Given dreams.

God gave you the dream and not someone else.

Quit expecting everyone else to see your dream.

Quit expecting everyone else to approve of your dream.

Stop the madness right now, God didn't give your Wife, your Husband, your Mamma or your Daddy your dream.

God give it to you, not them.

Understand that and you will not be swayed.

While I was taken back by the response of the man, I realized that God didn't give him the "God Made Millionaire" vision, he gave it to me.

It's impossible for him to see what I see.

But I digress.

Let me tell you a true story that illustrates why I believe that you are ALREADY a God Made Millionaire, but you just don't realize it yet.

There was a woman at a local flea market who came across a piece of costume jewelry.

She was actually drawn to the piece and LOVED how she felt when she wore the ring.

She felt like a Princess with the fake stone on her hand.

She paid her $13 for the ring and went on her way.

What followed was over 30 years of struggle.

For 30 years, she struggled each month to pay her bills but her ring would always give her comfort.

One day, she was at the market and a strange man took an interest in her ring and began to follow her.

Finally, the man confronts her and asks to take a closer look at her ring and she refuses and runs away.

Later, she leaves her home without the ring on and decides to go back and get the ring.

She wonders if maybe, there might be something more to the ring than she thought.

The woman then takes the ring to Sotheby's to be appraised.

The ring turned out to be a 26 custom-shaped white diamond that they are guessing was owned by Royalty at one time.

The antique shape and style of the diamond had hidden its real value all of these years and the rings true value was only recognized by that stranger who had happened upon the lady in the store.

The woman put the ring up at an auction where it was expected to sell for 450k and it ended up selling for 850k in US dollars.

For 30 years, this woman STRUGGLED every month to pay her bills...robbing "Peter to pay Paul" without realizing the ENTIRE time, she had FORTUNE on her finger that she didn't recognize the value of.

It took a complete stranger, someone else, to see the value that the woman was walking with.

Chances are you and I don't know each other and have not met yet.

I like to think that I am the stranger in that story, and I recognize the VALUE that God has placed in your heart, not on your finger.

I believe you have within you, a 6 and 7 figure dream already placed within you and this book and this chapter is going to be the key that spurs you to action to finally live the life that you have always dreamed of living.

For 30 years, this woman suffered when she didn't have to.

How many years have you walked around with a 6 and 7 figure dream that you didn't realize you had until a stranger came into your life via this chapter and recognized it?

That all stops the moment you recognize the VALUE of what has ALREADY been placed inside of you.

It's been there this entire time.

I want you to know something that I believe that I am talking directly to a God Made Millionaire...right now....Yes, YOU!

I believe that I'm talking to best-selling authors and you don't even know it yet.

I believe that I am talking to Grammy Award-winning songwriters and song singers and actors.

I believe that I am talking to Empire builders right now, you don't even know it.

Now, you have gifts and you have talents, you have abilities that are God-Given in you. You have a purpose and you've been playing small for too long. There's a generation of millionaires, of God Made Millionaires that God is going to raise up but not if you're dumb and you don't believe it.

Not if you talk yourself out of it, let me tell you something, your past doesn't determine your future. I don't care about how many things you've tried in the past and it didn't work.

What I care about is what God has given you to do; all you need to do is to FOCUS and take the action.

But listen; when you've been given an assignment, a destiny, you're responsible for it.

Where there's inspiration, there's obligation.

If I've inspired you in this chapter, then, there's an obligation that comes behind it, you got to take the action.

You got to do something today to build that Empire.

Get busy building your empire, you have no excuses. Stop playing small, you don't serve anybody by playing small alright and stop looking the natural.

Start looking at the supernatural where God operates.

# CHAPTER 4

## YOU'RE GOING TO HAVE TO SAY NO TO THE KING

If you're ever going to achieve your God-Given dream …You're going to have to learn to say no to the king.

You're going to have to learn how to say no to the King.

I'm talking about David when he took on the old giant Goliath, everybody is familiar with the story of David versus Goliath?

But I'm here to share with you some back story on that story that will help you with your God-Given dream.

Now I'm not talking about some little dream, I'm talking about something that God has purposed and called you to do and if you're ever going to get that done, you're going to have to learn to say no to the King.

You know when David was a young boy, he heard about Goliath, he was tending to the flock of sheep and he heard about this foul Philistine that was defying the armies of the Living God and he said, "Is there not a cause?"

He was willing to go fight because no one would take the fight to Goliath.

No man was willing to take the fight to Goliath, to the Giant in the land and David said: "is there not a cause?"

The cool thing is that, King Saul heard about the shepherd boy and called him into his court and he looked at him and he said "you're just yet a boy; this is a man of war from youth. You're just a child - you're not even an adult, how are you going to go in and take on this giant?"

David said to the King, "listen he said, when I was out with the sheep as the shepherd of those sheep, there is a lion and a bear that came and took one of the sheep and I went, not only did I get that sheep back but I took out the lion and the bear. I took him out, if you see me fight with a bear, you will pray for the bear."

Ok, he might not have said pray for the bear but hey, it would have been really cool if he had!

When he was telling the King of his past victories, what was he doing?

He was reminding the King and himself of the past victories that he had, where God had shown himself strong on his behalf.

There are times in your life when you take on a task, when you've been called to do something, what you've got to do is, first things first, you've got to remind yourself of some of the victories, of when God showed himself strong on your behalf, you've got to declare it, you've got to speak it out.

You've got to remind yourself that there are times in your life where if it had not been for the Lord on your side, you would have lost your mind years ago.

If it had not been for the Lord interceding and intervening in your life, in a situation, you would not have made it.

Like David, you are called by God to achieve your God-Given dream, when you're called and you're appointed to do it, you are called, and you are appointed to do it.

Period.

No one could talk David out of his gift, and no one should ever talk you out of yours!

Now, here's where David had to say no to the King, to fulfill his destiny.

The King has his armor put on David, had the breastplate, which was a chain mail, if you've been to a Renaissance Fair, you've seen the chain mail.

Goliath's chain mail, they say, weighed 125 pounds.

But King Saul had David equipped with his armor and David put on the armor and said "I've not proved this armor, it doesn't feel right to me."

He said no to the King, he said, "take this armor off", he said "no" to the King.

Just a stunning turn of events made even more stunning that a young boy was saying "no" to a powerful King!

Somebody that he would want favor with, somebody that you would think you know if the king is going to give you his armor, you don't want to offend the king.

And yet, David the child said no to the King!

**He knew his Destiny.**

Instead, he picked up five pebbles from the brook, but he said no to the King.

Think about this, the moment, the very moment that some people know about your God-Given dream, they're going to try to put some stuff on you, they're going to try to put some things on you, instead of a coat of chain mail armor, it will be their opinions, their beliefs, about how you are to achieve what God has anointed you to do.

And you've got to be strong enough to say no, keep your armor!

God has called me to do it, he's going to equip me to do it.

God's ways are not man's ways, man's ways was to put the armor on.

Man's way's was not to offend the king and say, "no, keep your armor", this wasn't pawn store type armor, this was the King's armor that he put on to David, the child, to go into battle against the Goliath, against the giant.

The giant that no man in the land wanted to face and yet he said, "no" and he took off the armor.

You've got to be able when you've been given the dream and others trying to put their opinions about how you're to achieve that dream and that's going to happen.

They're going have their opinions about how you're to do what you've been called to do and you've got to be able to say "no" to the King, and stand your ground that you have been called to do it.

While everyone in that land looked at the size of the Giant and David was the only one that looked at the size of his God, to intervene in that situation.

Regardless of what you may be going through today, regardless of how big your dream may be, regardless of how scary it may be, your God is bigger; your God is able to intervene on your behalf. If you look at my story, I tell my story, my "God Says When" story. I was literally in an ambulance dead for a minute and a half to two minutes, no heartbeat, no pulse and yet God intervened on my behalf and showed himself strong on my behalf and my message to you is, regardless of how dark the night is, regardless of how impossible your situation looks, God is able to intervene on your behalf.

It doesn't look any more hopeless than being dead for two minutes, yet God intervened on my behalf, and he can do it for you.

Man is not the final say-so, in your situation, or circumstance. Man doesn't have the final say, a man doesn't, a doctor
doesn't, a lawyer doesn't, a King doesn't.

Your God is able to right now, but you're going to have to
say no to the King.

If you're ever going to walk in your destiny, learn to say no to
the King!

God's given me this dream. He didn't give it to you, he gave
it to me for a reason and he's going to give me the way and the
knowledge to do it.

Just say "NO" to the Kings in your life!

# CHAPTER 5

## FROM CAVEMAN TO BILLIONAIRES

I want you to realize and I want you to understand that I firmly believe that we are in the midst of the greatest transfer of wealth our generation has ever seen.

We are in the midst of one of the greatest transfers of wealth our generation has ever seen for God's people and I will tell you that and I will say this to you unapologetically, this only applies to you, if you're not dumb.

If you're not dumb and you make a poor choice not to believe what I am telling you, you can stay broke.

I want to share a story with you that illustrate this point.

A few years ago, there were two brothers from the country of Hungary, and they lived in a cave.

They were destitute brothers, so they did what they could to get by.

Now, in that region of the world, in that country, they have caves with impressive lighting, so I believe it's over 200 caves in that area, and they found themselves "broke, busted, and can't be trusted" and living in a cave selling candy and salvaging junk to survive on a daily basis.

And these two brothers, unbeknownst to them, had a grandmother that was incredibly wealthy, so wealthy she was worth over 6.2 billion dollars. (that's billion with a B)

They had issues with and were estranged from their mother when their mother passed away.

They were never in contact with their Mother or Father.

So, these brothers were both living in a cave when their maternal grandmother passes away and leaves them a fortune.

**A 6.2 billion-dollar fortune.**

They had a sister here in the States as well that could lay claim or had a claim to the fortune.

Overnight, they had no idea that their fortunes had changed living in that cave, that they were now the rightful heirs to over 6.2 billion dollars.

This happens to be a true story.

You can google "caveman billionaires" and you can research it for yourself as it's been covered all over the international press a few years ago, but I want to ask you a question…At what point in time did the caveman brothers become billionaires?

I present to you that those brothers became billionaires the moment they came out of their cave to claim the fortune that was rightfully theirs.

They had to leave the comfort of what they've always known, to leave that cave to lay claim to their fortune.

I am coming to you in this chapter as God's litigator, as God's attorney, so to speak, even though I am not an attorney, nor do I play one on TV.

I am officially informing you that you are heir to a FORTUNE that you didn't even know about...until this exact moment.

It's up to you to believe the word that is being brought forth to you and leave the cave you have been hiding in.

The cave where you play life safe while you struggle...

Every.

Single.

Day.

The cave is a safe place for you.

There is no judgement in your cave, only the contempt and disgust you have for living a life that you KNOW you were destined to live, but are not.

If you are reading this chapter at this precise moment in time, let me cut to the chase and tell you that there's something that you have been called to do, there's a purpose that you've been given a mandate to carry out, that you've been given from the Lord to do and only you can do it but it's going to involve that you believe it and that you leave that cave you have been hiding out in all of these years.

Some of you have been in a cave for years and you're used to living in that cave because it's comfortable and it's safe.

But God is calling you to a higher level, he's calling you to a level of success and prosperity that you don't even realize, it's there waiting for you outside the cave door.

**God GREATEST wealth and riches are NEVER found on the safety of the shoreline or security of the cave.**

If you are ever going to walk in Supernatural Wealth and Prosperity and see that God-given dream become a reality in your life, you are going to have to leave the cave and head to the deep waters.

Listen, ladies and gentlemen, for those two cavemen brothers, their past didn't matter, none of that mattered, it didn't invalidate their fortune, it didn't but let me share this with you, that the Lord is a gentleman, God is a gentleman, God will never force you to come out of the cave, God will never madate for you to leave that cave. It's going to be up to you, YOU have a voice that deserves to be heard! I am speaking to "God Made Millionaires" that are reading this chapter.

Let me explain something to you, my life is lived by divine appointment, there are some of you that never look at these type of books, but something has compelled you to read this book at this precise moment in time.

Only God could orchestrate this precise moment in your life.

Some of you reading this book have NEVER once, read this type of book before and yet, here you are.

I present to you that you are NOT here by accident.

You are here by divine appointment and you are being called to a level of wealth, prosperity and success that you can't even imagine, but it's going to require that you believe and that you come out of your cave.

You know you have a voice that people need to hear!

I am speaking to God Made Millionaires...RIGHT NOW!

I am speaking to best-selling authors RIGHT NOW!

I'm speaking to singers and artists RIGHT NOW!

I am speaking to EMPIRE builders in business, RIGHT NOW!

I am speaking to POWERFUL Men and Women of God who God has called but you had a setback and you have been hiding in the cave, licking your wounds, come out RIGHT NOW!

It's time for YOU to leave the cave RIGHT NOW!

I decree wealth and prosperity into your life.

I decree it right now, that dream, that God-given dream that you've been given will come to pass once you leave the cave...RIGHT NOW!

# CHAPTER 6

## SOMETIMES IN LIFE, YOU HAVE TO MAKE A STATEMENT!

O ne afternoon, I had to run a couple of errands and I actually drove past the ambulance.

Not just any ambulance but THE Ambulance.

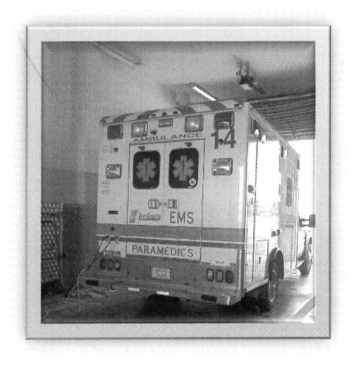

This is the picture of the actual ambulance that I died in back in 2012. For those of you that are not familiar with my story, I had a sudden cardiac arrest and I was actually dead for a period of between 1.5 minutes to 2 minutes before I was revived and brought back to life.

The survival rate for an "out of hospital" sudden cardiac arrest is less than 1%...9 out of 10 guys are not going to make it. If you are fortunate enough to survive, you're usually going to have some sort of mental deficit because of the lack of oxygen and blood flow to the brain and your vital organs.

And yet, I came out without spot or blemish.

As I passed that ambulance that day, it reminded me of when I was first released from the hospital.

I remember that my wife told me that the doctors had advised her to keep a close eye on me because of the trauma that I went through.

You know, it's interesting when people ask me whether I had a near-death experience?

**No, I always tell them, I didn't have a near-death experience, I actually died.**

There's a difference in my opinion.

So, I remember my wife telling me when we got home from the hospital that the doctors had advised her to keep an eye on me because of the traumatic things that had happened to me.

The doctors shared with my wife that there was a very good likelihood that I would go through a major bout of depression because of the trauma that I went through, I mean they shocked me twice (2x) to bring me back to life.

The doctors said he's going to be prone to serious, serious depression.

I remember telling my wife, you know they're talking about the wrong guy. When I was a much younger man, if you told me I couldn't do something, I wouldn't just only do it once, I would do it twice. The first time to prove to you that I could do it, and the second time too, just in case you missed it the first time.

So, the fact that they had said that was what was going to happen to me was all I needed to prove those doctors wrong.

But here's an interesting story for you, in those first few weeks after my sudden cardiac arrest occurred, any time I was out and I saw an ambulance, I would start to get emotional.

It would really impact me on a <u>core level</u> where I would get misty-eyed and start to get a little tear in my eyes.

I also could not watch TV shows, especially if I would see a scene similar to what had happened to me.

It would just get to me, I'd have to just get up and leave.

To this day, I cannot comfortably watch a TV show that is dealing with that issue.

Here is my point.

We all have had traumatic incidents happen in our life, maybe not as traumatic as what had happened in my life, but we've all been through trauma whether it's personal, whether it's your health, whether it's your family, or whether its financial trauma.

I'm here to tell you today, that there comes a time in your life where you have to make a statement.

You have to draw the line in the sand, you have to say enough is enough and you have to rise up, out of that situation.

You have to rise up, out of that circumstance.

How you handle the moments of decision after the trauma will determine your destiny.

I'm convinced of the fact you've got to plant your flag; you've got to make a statement.

You've got to make a statement.

I remember it was about three months after the incident, I was at a local grocery store and I saw the ambulance that I had died in.

I saw it parked in the local parking lot and I remember walking up to the paramedics and letting them know. "You know that ambulance you're driving, I died in it about three months ago"

I remember the shock on their face, they said, "Sir, you have no idea what a miracle you are." They said, " People that were in your condition, we take them to the hospital but they don't walk out of the hospital, the fact that you're walking is a miracle."

They ended by telling me that I had overcome Powerball type odds to survive that event.

And I thanked them for their service, and I walked out to the parking lot, still with that wound fresh in my mind.

I remember walking up to that ambulance and knocking on the side of that ambulance. I knocked on the side of it and I said, "I'm still here and I'm still standing."

Now I don't care who heard it or who saw it.

There are times in your life you've got to make a statement.

You've got to draw a line in the sand, and you've got to say "enough is enough".

Some of you have been living in certain situations and circumstances with certain events occurring in your life in the past and you've allowed those events in your past to rob you of your future.

For some reason, today is your day to draw that line in the sand.

Today is your day to say enough is enough.

You've got to take the stand; you've got to make your statement.

See, as somebody that is building an empire, I have got to

make a statement every single day.

And if I'm going to make a statement, it's going to be something that's powerful.

**Every time I wear my God Made Millionaire shirt, I am making a POWERFUL statement.**

*These are not my arms in this picture but I do wear this shirt...haha*

A POWERFUL Decree.

So, you've got to make a statement.

Every.

Single.

Day.

I'll close this chapter by telling you about Michael Jordan of the Chicago Bulls which had one of the best teams in basketball.

What you don't know is, the practices that he (Michael Jordan) had to go through were harder than the actual games.

He made a statement every single day in practice.

Those practices were so intense that when it was time to play the actual games, those games were a walk in the park.

Champions make statements every single day.

Your past doesn't equal your future.

It's time to get over that stuff, it's time to draw the line in the sand and say enough is enough.

You're not going to be denied your dream, your vision.

What you've been given to do, it's up to you to achieve it.

Plant your flag, stake your claim and make a statement!

# CHAPTER 7

## WHAT YOU SEE IS WHAT YOU GET!

It is one of the most profound spiritual laws of success that exists in the universe.

What You See Is What You Get!

Now, I'm dating myself when I tell you this, but I don't know if you remember the great comedian Flip Wilson?

That was his famous tagline, and little did he know, it was one of the most powerful spiritual laws of success.

Nowadays, you have people that will say what you see is what you get and they're unapologetic, and maybe they're snapping their fingers.

Same phrase, different meaning today.

But what you see is really what you get, if you are ever going to transform your life, if you're ever going to transform your finances, which is a very important topic for a lot of people, "their finances", you're going to have to train your vision on what you can't see in the natural.

It's just a fact.

You see a gentleman driving a Cadillac and you say, "I just could never see myself driving a car like that."

How often have you said that yourself?

Or "I could never see myself living in a house like that"

**What you see is what you get.**

If you can't see yourself living in a house like that, you aren't going to have to worry about it because **it isn't going to happen.**

The first million-dollar company that I built; I saw that as a million-dollar company before we ever did a dollar in business.

I saw that before anybody else did.

Steve Jobs saw Apple before anybody else saw Apple.

Bill Gates saw Microsoft before anybody else saw Microsoft.

You've got to develop your spiritual eyes.

There's a generation of millionaires, of God Made Millionaires that God is going to raise up but not if you only focus on what you can "see" at the moment.

You've got to develop your spiritual eyes.

When God gives you a dream, when God gives you a vision, you're the only one that can see it. Your spouse cannot see it. Your mommy can't see it. Your daddy can't see it.

What you see is what you get.

How many times have you ever watched a movie and then dreamed about that movie? Years ago, there was a movie with snakes on a plane. And people watched this movie and then, that night they dreamt about snakes.

 Now has that ever happened to you?

You're like, that's the goofiest movie I've ever seen. Snakes on a plane, but then that night, you dream about snakes.

The word of God says, be renewed by the transforming of your mind, your mind is transformed by what you're seeing in your mind. It starts there.

I want to tell you a story about a man named Ray.

This is a true story and I have changed the first name to protect the innocent.

Ray came to me because he wanted me to personally coach him how to invest in real estate, which back then since I had a best-selling program on that topic, a lot of people wanted me to coach them, so I agreed to coach Jim.

On his first coaching call with me, Jim let me know, he didn't like his job. He was not shy about letting me know he hated his job. And the reason he had hired me as a coach is because he wanted to make real estate investing his full-time source of income, wanted to do it, and was committed to doing it right.

A couple of days after our first coaching call, I was sitting in my office and the phone rings and it's Ray and he's in tears. I said, "what happened?" *I'm thinking, who died?* And I said, "My God Ray, what is wrong?" And Ray says, "I've lost my job". I was fired today. I said, "wait, hold on. What?" I couldn't compute what he had just said: " you were fired today?"

"Yes, and I don't know what I'm going to do" was his response through the tears.

I said, "wait a minute. Wait a minute, man. Let me get this right. That job last week that you told me that you hated, that you despised. You're telling me that you were fired from that job and you're calling me up in tears." He replied me and said, "That's the job". I responded, "You're telling me that you lost the one thing that you hate so much."

"I don't know what I'm going to do. I don't know what I'm going to do." was Ray's feeble response.

What you see is what you get.

In my mind what I saw was a perfect opportunity to walk in his dream of being a full-time real estate investor.

I saw no more excuses for him to walk in that destiny.

Nothing to hold him back, nothing to shackle him.

**All he could see was financial ruin.**

In this life, what you see is what you get.

The first company that we built to a multi-million-dollar status, my partner terminated the partnership and told me he was keeping the company.

This was a man I trusted like a Father figure.

My life changed in a moment, in an instant.

I remember looking at my wife Vickie after I had gotten the news that you own a $10 million company one day, and the next day you don't.

We had every nickel, every dollar invested in that company and one day it was gone.

And Vickie, ashen grey in her face, looked at me and she said, "what are we going to do? What are we going to do?"

I looked at her without hesitation and I said, "We're going to invest in real estate. That's what we're going to do".

I remember Vickie in shock saying "oh, really? Oh really?"

"Yes, we're going to invest in real estate."

That's precisely what I did.

Within 90 days, I had my first deal. Within 24 hours of the first deal, I had my second deal and the rest is history.

What you see is what you get.

How many times is your vision been impacted by somebody who never had the vision?

Here's the thing, sweet pea, God didn't give the vision to somebody else. He gave you the vision. He gave you the vision, not somebody else. Don't expect somebody else to have the vision God gave you. Don't expect somebody else to have the vision or understand the vision that he's planted in you.

**What you see is what you get, what you see, not what you deserve.**

What you see is what you get.

How about the story of the "Tower of Babel" in the Bible?

You have people who are building a tower to the heavens and do you know what the word of God says in reference to that?

God said there's nothing that is impossible to these people with their imagination.

So, he had to confound their languages. He had to change up their languages.

What you see is what you get. Let that soak in, let that marinate in your spirit.

What are you seeing?

What you see is what you get.

What are you viewing?

What are you seeing?

What are you putting in your mind before you go to bed?

I'll tell you what, I won't watch those horror movies, I don't watch them. No Way. Vickie was watching something the other night, it had spiders on it, and sure enough, at three o'clock in the morning, she wakes me up because she dreamed about spiders!

What you see is what you get.

How powerful is that?

You have control over what you see.

You have control over what you see and what you see is what you get.

# CHAPTER 8

## A BLESSING TO ALL NATIONS!

You know in these last few chapters that I've done, I've actually spoken quite a bit about building an empire, and one of the reasons that I speak about this is, that's what I personally think about, every single day, building an empire.

I believe that we are in the greatest time to be alive in our lifetime, and I believe that God's people are getting ready to experience the greatest transfer of wealth our generation has ever seen.

It's going to happen for God's people, and it will happen for some that read this book, but not if you're dumb, and not if you don't believe that it can happen.

The Word of God says, "my people are destroyed for a lack of knowledge" and that "where there's no vision, the people perish"

I'm a huge believer of having a vision and keeping that vision before me at all times.

One of the declarations that I've made for years over my life and over my business is that I am a blessing to all nations.

I am a blessing to all nations.

I don't have and I've never had some small-minded "dinky donkey dream.

I've always been world-class in my thinking.

I've always been global in my thinking and it's interesting because in my office I have on my wall, a framed picture of the world.

Every day I'm raising my hands towards that board of the Nations and declaring that I am a Blessing to all Nations.

The only failure in a man with dreams is broken focus.

That's when you get distracted somewhere along the line, somebody somewhere convinced you that there was a better "plan B" for your life than what God had planned for you.

**The only reason that you've failed is because of a broken focus.**

Never let anyone talk you out of your gift or God-given dream.

God's not calling you to some dinky donkey small-minded dream, he's calling you to build an empire, a Global Empire.

Now, for some of you, that may not be true, but for most reading this book, it is true.

You will be a BLESSING to All Nations!

Declare it and DECREE it!

It's true, but for those that still doubt my words, let me share with you some ways you could be a blessing to all nations.

There are some of you that you know you've been called to write a book and yet you've done nothing with that calling.

Do you realize that you could write a book and you can publish it on Amazon, and it could be available globally, worldwide, in a hundred and fifty countries?

Do you realize it you could put a product together on a website and sell that product to over a hundred different nations?

You're talking to the guy that after having his first website built, had customers and clients in over a hundred different nations.

This book that are you now reading, the very month that it was released, it had 3 major TV interviews set up for the media tour.

1 was national, seen in over 180 markets across the country, reaching more than 50 million homes.

The other 2 TV interviews were seen in 200 Nations.

Before I started doing this, I was not known by anyone.

Think I am kidding about this stuff?

I am not.

**This one chapter can TRANSFORM YOUR world and the Nations!**

How about this one, do you remember the lady who recorded herself putting on that Chewbacca mask on and was laughing so hard and authentically, her video went global worldwide.

She was a blessing to all nations by giving people the gift of laughter and she received endorsement deals as a result.

There are some of you that have the gift of music in you and one YouTube video can go global nationwide; you can be a blessing to all nations.

You have no excuses with all of the social media platforms that we have nowadays, but it's never going to happen if you don't think it's going to happen.

God is looking for his people to step up into their destiny, God is looking for his people to step up to what he has called you to be, and to do, and to walk in that dream.

I'm telling you right now, God does not deal in "dinky donkey" dreams or small dreams.

Stop playing small.

Stop dreaming small.

Start declaring and decreeing that you are a Blessing to All Nations...because you are!

# CHAPTER 9

## THERE IS NO SUCH THING AS A SELF-MADE MILLIONAIRE

People see me speak on TV and will often remark on "how natural I am at speaking"

Nothing could be further from the truth.

What most of you are not aware of is the fact that up until the time I was five years old, I had a major speech defect that resulted in my not being able to speak.

Literally, I couldn't utter a word.

The only people that would really understand me were my mother and my father. The other kids were incredibly cruel to me and make fun of me in school so much that I remember coming home the first day of school in tears and told my dad that I was not going to go back to school. My Father convinced me otherwise.

My father was a blue-collar worker and he refused to take no for an answer when it came to me and my speech defect. He took me from specialist to specialist and one specialist said that I was mentally retarded, that's what they used to say back in those days, that terminology. Another one said that I was deaf and would not be able to ever speak again.

My father never accepted those Doctors opinions. He would firmly say that there is a Doctor in Chicago that can fix my son and I am going to find them.

And find him he did.

At 5 years of age, I had major surgery and that was followed by a major speech therapy until I got to the 4th grade.

Fast forward to my last day of schooling, I was selected to give the graduation speech by my classmates and I got a standing ovation.

Here it is, 30 plus years later and they still talk about that speech and can even recite one of the lines from the speech.

Only God can orchestrate such a turnaround.

My first day of school, coming home in tears because I was made fun of and the last day of school, being selected to speak and getting a standing ovation from my classmates.

In spite of any success that I may have, there's still that five-year-old boy still within me.

You know the one that was made fun of in school and I've never forgotten that, that five-year-old boy.

When I got out of high school, I was incredibly fortunate

enough to work for two millionaires, John A. Oremus and his son Jack Oremus. They owned the biggest ready-mix company in the Midwest. John A. Oremus actually founded the company and his son Jack grew the company to incredible heights with his family.

They saw something in me, and they took me under their wing. I had more heart than talent, but they saw something, and they mentored me at a very young age about business and building an empire.

I've never met a man that walks the face of the earth that is my father's equal and I've never met anyone in business as a businessman that is Jack Oremus's equal or John Oremus's equal, they don't exist.

These two high school-educated men that were legendary absolutely built an empire and yet were so humble, they lovingly sowed into my life to such a degree that 30 years afterwards, I still have a picture of Jack and John in my office in honor of the impact that they made into my life.

I think it's important that you know that when you look at someone and you see the signs of success, you can easily see the houses, the cars, the businesses that they have, but what you don't see is the story behind the success and the reality is that, there is no such thing as a "self-made millionaire"

Such a thing doesn't exist.

There is no such thing as a self-made millionaire.

I stand on the shoulders of my mother and of my father; I stand on the shoulders of Jack Oremus and John A. Oremus, who taught me how to build an empire. They didn't just teach me verbally, they showed me by their actions how to build a successful business. I stand on their shoulders.

I stand on the shoulders of therapist's, the therapists that took me under their wing and literally taught me how to speak.

I stand on the shoulders of my pastor in Chicago, Pastor Dan Willis; he taught me how to be a Christian man.

I stand on the shoulders of so many people, so many people.

It irritates me whenever I hear the term, self-made millionaire.

## United States of America

### United States Patent and Trademark Office

## GOD MADE MILLIONAIRE

Reg. No. 4,661,127

Registered Dec. 23, 2014

Int. Cl.: 35

SERVICE MARK

PRINCIPAL REGISTER

NEW LIFE VISION,LLC (FLORIDA LIMITED LIABILITY COMPANY)
1616 W. CAPE CORAL PARKWAY,#231
CAPE CORAL, FL 33914

FOR: ONLINE RETAIL STORE SERVICES FEATURING BOOKS, SHIRTS, HATS, SCREEN SAVERS, CALENDARS, COFFEE CUPS, MUGS, IN CLASS 35 (U.S. CLS. 100, 101 AND 102).

FIRST USE 10-23-2014; IN COMMERCE 10-23-2014

THE MARK CONSISTS OF STANDARD CHARACTERS WITHOUT CLAIM TO ANY PARTICULAR FONT, STYLE, SIZE, OR COLOR.

SN 86-247,039, FILED 4-9-2014.

LIEF MARTIN, EXAMINING ATTORNEY

Michelle K. Lee
Deputy Director of the United States
Patent and Trademark Office

I actually trademarked the term "God Made Millionaire" because it means so much more to me, it's personal.

I've been using that term since 2003 and by the time that I am done, the world will know that there is no such thing as a Self-Made Millionaire.

Now I want to close by telling you a story that illustrates this point.

Back in the fifteenth century, in a tiny village near Nuremberg, lived a family with eighteen children. Eighteen!

In order to keep food on the table for this mob, the father and head of the household, a goldsmith by profession, worked almost eighteen hours a day at his trade and any other paying chore he could find in the neighborhood.

Despite their seemingly hopeless condition, two of the elder children, Albrecht and Albert, had a dream. They both wanted to pursue their talent for art, but they knew fully well that their father would never be financially capable of sending either of them to Nuremberg to study at the Academy.

After many long discussions at night in their crowded bed, the two boys finally worked out a pact. They would toss a coin. The loser would go down into the nearby mines and, with his earnings, support his brother while he attended the academy. Then, when that brother who won the toss completed his studies, in four years, he would support the other brother at the academy, either with sales of his artwork or, if necessary, also by laboring in the mines.

They tossed a coin on a Sunday morning after church. Albrecht Durer won the toss and went off to Nuremberg.

Albert went down into the dangerous mines and, for the next four years, financed his brother, whose work at the academy was almost an immediate sensation. Albrecht's etchings, his woodcuts, and his oils were far better than those of most of his professors, and by the time he graduated, he was beginning to earn considerable fees for his commissioned works.

When the young artist returned to his village, the Durer family held a festive dinner on their lawn to celebrate Albrecht's triumphant homecoming. After a long and memorable meal, punctuated with music and laughter, Albrecht rose from his honored position at the head of the table to drink a toast to his beloved brother for the years of sacrifice that had enabled Albrecht to fulfill his ambition. His closing words were, "And now, Albert, blessed brother of mine, now, it's your turn. Now you can go to Nuremberg to pursue your dream, and I will take care of you."

All heads turned in eager expectation to the far end of the table where Albert sat, tears streaming down his pale face, shaking his lowered head from side to side while he sobbed and repeated, over and over, "No... no... no... no."

Finally, Albert rose and wiped the tears from his cheeks. He glanced down the long table at the faces he loved, and then, holding his hands close to his right cheek, he said softly, "No, brother. I cannot go to Nuremberg. It is too late for me. Look... Look what four years in the mines have done to my hands! The bones in every finger have been smashed at least once, and lately,

I have been suffering from arthritis so badly in my right hand that I cannot even hold a glass to return your toast, much less make delicate lines on parchment or canvas with a pen or a brush. No brother... for me, it is too late."

More than 450 years have passed since then. At the moment, Albrecht Durer's hundreds of masterful portraits, pen and silver-point sketches, water colors, charcoals, woodcuts, and copper engravings hang in every great museum in the world, but the odds are great that you, like most people, are familiar with only one of Albrecht Durer's works. More than merely being familiar with it, you may very well have a reproduction hanging in your home or office.

One day, in order to pay homage to Albert for all that he had sacrificed, Albrecht Durer painstakingly drew his brother's abused hands with palms together and thin fingers stretched skyward. He simply called his powerful drawing "Hands," but the entire world almost immediately opened their hearts to his great masterpiece and renamed his tribute of love "The Praying Hands." The next time you see a copy of that touching creation, take a second look. Let it be your reminder, that no one - ever makes it alone!

When I tell you there is no such thing as a self-made millionaire, I mean it with every breath in my body.

It's my mission and my purpose to let the world know, there is no such thing as a "self-made millionaire". We all stand on the shoulders of somebody, we all do, you don't make it to the top by yourself, no one does.

# CHAPTER 10

## NEVER ALLOW OTHERS TO DEFINE YOU!

I am in a very competitive media and publishing business. It's highly competitive in that business. And yet I'm incredibly successful in that business model. And part of the reason is that I don't allow others to define who I am.

I want you to realize that not everyone brings to the table what you bring to the table.

**God is a creator. He's not a duplicator.**

You are unique, you have a unique set of skill sets and talents and abilities.

No one does what you do.

I had a client a couple of weeks ago, the client said to me, well, in reference to some advice and counsel that I provided to him.

He said. "Well, I've heard that before."

And I said. "Well, you may have heard it before, but you never heard it from me. Because I'm the one telling you what you need to do."

When somebody tries to say to you in your business, that there are people "just like you," that does what you do. I always correct them.

"That's not true, you've never met anybody like me in this business that does what I do. Now, you may run across other people that provide media and publishing services. But you'll never ever speak to anybody like me that's providing those services."

People are very quick to want to box you into their frame of thinking or try to put you into a box with other people. And you've got to understand your value and your worth and your uniqueness.

Nobody and I mean nobody does what you do.

**Your Wealth Is Found In Your DIFFERENCES, NOT How You Are Like Everyone Else in the Market!**

Never allow anyone to put you in a box and say this is what you do, or this is what you bring, or worse than that, you're like everybody else.

In 5 years, our publishing division has created over 100 best-selling authors.

I have clients out there, that are at the top of the food chain in their industries. Highly competitive industries and spaces, they come to me for my counsel and my advice.

So, when somebody comes to me and says, "You're just like this other guy who is doing media and publishing", that simply isn't the truth.

Understand this, no one does what you do.

No one brings to the table what you bring with your life experience, your talents and your abilities.

I realize there's a bunch of you that actually love my content.

But I'm not for everybody, but I am for somebody.

Stop trying to please everybody. Because you're not for everybody but you are for somebody.

When I started doing my "FOX4" TV segments, at the end of the segment, I would put on my sunglasses and "mean mug" the camera.

My co-host would get in on the fun.

Now 1 of 2 things is going to happen because of this.

Some people are going to see the segment and think that I am so unprofessional, that they would NEVER do business with someone so unprofessional.

Here is the thing, I would NEVER do business with them either.

The other group of people will look at that segment and will LOVE a guy that is so fearless on TV and has the confidence to throw his shades on and mean mug the camera and they will say that I am their man.

I will never sacrifice my personality for someone that would never become a client of mine anyway.

Recently, I listened to Elvis, the greatest singer that ever lived, he sang a song called "Let It Be" by the Beatles. And I have news for you, even though Elvis is like the greatest singer ever; I preferred the Beatles version of "Let It Be".

They own that version.

I mean Elvis can sing it, but it doesn't matter, it's still not as good as the authentic version of the Beatles.

You're not a duplicate, so be original, and be authentic in this marketplace.

And the right people will resonate with that messaging.

There is nothing worse in the marketplace then someone trying to be something or someone that they are not.

# CHAPTER 11

## GOD GIVES MILLION DOLLAR DREAMS NOT MILLION DOLLAR BLUEPRINTS

We've all had the moments where you've been given a million-dollar idea. I know you have, the clouds have parted and you got divine inspiration and you know it's a million-dollar idea, but then, you don't do anything with it, or you get overwhelmed or life takes over or you get "realistic " and you don't do anything.

God has not called you to be realistic, God is a supernatural God. But here's the key, you've got to take action.

**God Gives Million Dollar Dreams NOT Million Dollar Blueprints!**

God never gives you the second step until you take the first step.

But if you are like most people, you want all 10 steps handed to you on a silver platter, God simply doesn't operate that way.

By faith, you must take the first step to be given the second step.

I see this in our publishing business all of the time.

God has called someone to write a book, but nothing ever happens with that dream because of so many different excuses.

Usually, people talk themselves out of their dream because they don't feel qualified or simply because they have never done it before.

People who are not serious and simply put their toes in the water NEVER have divine providence move on their behalf.

But as soon as someone becomes committed to their dream and takes the first step, miracles begin to happen.

**Commitment is the launching pad of miracles.**

Until a man or woman is truly committed to their God-given dream, they are simply wasting time and fooling themselves.

I see this transformation occur in our publishing clients all of the time.

The biggest concern before they become a client is "what will I write?"

After they are truly committed and become a client, then, it's like a literal download of information floods their brains and they get revelation and insights they never would have gotten had they not made the commitment with our publishing firm.

That's the magic of commitment.

**Miracles follow commitment; they never show up before that.**

I really want to do a deep dive in this chapter and share with you, my personal experience with this topic as it relates to the media side (TV) of our business.

God gave me a dream to get involved in TV, but not the blueprint.

A lot of my publishing clients would ask me if I could feature them on TV after we had published their books.

I had ZERO connections in the TV space, but I had a dream.

My dream was to have a franchise TV business segment where I could feature my publishing clients and their leadership on the segment.

When I say franchise segment, I mean a segment that was exclusive to our publishing and media firm.

No one but our clients can be placed on that segment, hence the term "franchise segment".

Again, this was a pretty big dream because I had no connections in the TV industry.

I saw how people LOVED Shark Tank and how 1 TV appearance could change the fortunes of a client or company overnight, and this is what I wanted for my clients.

So I made the commitment to seeing this dream come true.

The TV industry is very fast-moving and unforgiving.

Calls and emails were not returned.

One day, I stopped by my local FOX station and requested to speak to someone.

That morning, I signed a 1-year contract for my franchise business segment "Business Leaders Spotlight"

Even though the segment only aired locally in my market, I had clients fly in from all over the USA and the world to appear on the segment.

After two (2) successful years of running our franchise segment, an opportunity arose to have our segments featured on a nationally syndicated talk that is aired in 180 markets across the country, many of them with network affiliates like ABC, CBS, NBC, FOX, and CW reaching more than 50 million homes.

So now, we can feature our clients on a national level, just like Shark Tank, on our franchise segment, "Business Leaders Spotlight" TV segment.

But this would have never happened if I was not committed to this dream.

It never would have happened if I demanded that God give me the blueprint to make this happen.

I never saw how any of this was possible, but I didn't need to.

All I needed was to take the first step and go to the TV studio that morning.

Truth be told, even me getting that meeting and signing that 1-year contract that morning was a miracle as most TV stations are secure fortresses nowadays.

Any nut job that wants to get on TV simply has to do something stupid at a TV station to get on TV, so they do NOT prefer on-site visits, but phone calls and emails.

I could have easily quit when my phone calls and emails were not returned, but that is where commitment comes in.

**My commitment carried me when it didn't look like it was going to happen.**

And had I not been faithful with the first step, the second step, the National TV show would have never occurred.

Please stop shooting yourself in the foot and sabotaging your God-given dreams by wanting to have it "all figured out" or having "your ducks in a row"

That's not how God operates.

What you end up doing is reducing the size of your dream so you can "figure it all out"

God doesn't give small dreams, at least he doesn't give small dreams to you, or you would not be reading this book.

No one gave me the blueprint to do TV, but I have it now and my clients enjoy the benefits of this.

I now have access to a National TV platform that will help others and make their God-Given dreams come true.

But God was not finished with the TV blueprint.

The first step was FOX4, the second step was the National TV show, and the 3rd step was access to feature our clients on a faith-based talk show that is seen in 200 different Nations, and is produced by the largest faith-based media company in the world

**Only God could orchestrate something like this.**

Once again, because I was faithful in taking the first and second step, the third step was provided, and our clients are already enjoying the fruit of that commitment by being featured on a faith-based TV show that airs in 200 nations.

Do you see how this thing works now?

When you are faithful to do what God has called you to do, you are going to be in a position to help others do what God has called THEM to do.

By the way, the way that you know it is a God-given dream is when you have no clue how it's going to happen.

If you have it all figured out, then I can tell you with 100% certainty that you are not dreaming big enough.

Take the first step today, however small of a step that it may seem like, and make sure you are 100% committed to seeing your God driven dream become a reality and you will know divine providence move on your behalf, but only if you are committed.

# CHAPTER 12

## LIVING LIFE ON YOUR TERMS!

One of the most defining moments in my life actually came very close to not happening. Well, not very close, but let me share the story with you.

20 years ago, Vickie and I made a decision to move here to our dream home in Cape Coral, Florida from Chicago, and that move was NOT a popular move with our family and friends in Chicago.

There was intense, and I do mean serious intense opposition to this move down to Florida.

There was a lot of pressure on me, not to make that move to come here where we didn't know anybody at all. No family. No friends. Didn't even know if we would like living here or not.

I've always lived my life from a young man, not doing what YOU think that I should do. I'm always going to make a decision based on what I think is best at the time. I call that living life on your terms, and not somebody else's terms.

Now, even in spite of that intense opposition, we came down

here to Florida.

It was a defining moment in our life.

It literally changed the course of our life, and it could have never happened if I bowed to that pressure of what good people, loving people were whispering in my ear about not making this move.

But it turned out to be the correct move.

Folks, this happens quite a bit.

There are so many people right now, reading this chapter, you are kidding yourself because you're not living life on your terms.

You're living life according to what other people expectations are.

That's not called living life on your terms.

If you will remember this, and you never forget it, it will carry you for the rest of your life. And it's this. No matter what you decide to do, whatever decision you're going to make, there's going to be people that find reasons to doubt that decision.

There's going to be people that oppose that decision.

You've got to do what is right for you.

That's right. Because if you make the wrong decision, and you base it on this person down the street or based on a spouse or a relative, and it turns out to be the wrong decision, well, you can't blame them because you alone are accountable.

You alone are responsible for that decision.

I occasionally do Facebook live videos and like to have fun doing them.

I have had well-meaning people reach out to me and say "TC, if only you were more serious on those videos that you do, how do you expect people to take you seriously with your videos?"

My response never changes.

Listen, I live life on my terms.

**I don't live my life the way you think that I should live my life. I simply don't. You shouldn't either folks.**

My Wife Vickie is a classic example of this.

Sometimes, God-Given Dreams do not involve money or building a 6 or 7 figure empire.

My wife has always had a heart of love and compassion towards people.

She wanted to do some type of work in nursing.

Now, as her husband, I don't want her to work for anyone.

That's why I do what I do.

But for years now, Vickie was on the elevator that I spoke about in Chapter 2 and lets me push the button to the floors that we both travel to.

One day, she pushed the button herself, the one called CNA.

She went and was hired at a company that helps seniors with In-home care.

She quickly rose to the #1 requested CNA in that company.

Her clients LOVE her and so did the company.

But Vickie had other ideas.

She secured the insurance required to operate and went into business to offer private duty.

This is her ministry and her heartbeat.

Nothing makes her happier than helping those that she cares for with dignity and a whole bunch of LOVE.

Although Vickie is paid very well, she doesn't do what she does for the money.

**It's what she feels that she has been put on earth to do.**

It's as simple as that.

I could NEVER do what My wife does because that is not my calling or gift.

So, God-given dreams are not just about the money.

I didn't understand her decision to go this route, and I was not on board with this decision, but Vickie knew exactly what she wanted and pushed that button called CNA in that elevator and she could not be happier, and really now, so am I.

I am so very proud of my wife for doing what she does and her accomplishments.

Now, I know her story will inspire other women around the world to follow their God given dreams.

That it is never too late to see that God given dream come to pass.

So often, people make a decision, and here's what happens. You make a decision that you're going to change your life. Now, this is going to require that you get outside of your comfort zone; what I talked about all throughout this book. But you make that decision, and then you let other people know about it. Bamm! Immediately that opposition comes into play. Those opposing forces come into play. At the end of the day, you got to take personal accountability and responsibility for your life.

If you have a dream that God has given you, that's your dream. You're responsible for that dream, and if he's giving you the dream, he's giving you the ability to make that happen. But, it's not going to happen if you listen to these people chirping in your ears, and trying to destroy you.

I'm going to tell you something, they can be very well-meaning people, but you've got to "know that you know" that you're on the right pathway.

You've got to know this too, that any change that is going to be real in your life is going to require you to get outside of your comfort zone.

# CHAPTER 13

## GOD IS NOT SENDING YOU A CHECK IN THE MAIL MAILBOX MILLIONAIRE MENTALITY

For most faith-based people reading this book, this will be the most important chapter you will read in this book.

Most church people have been taught how to sow a seed.

Faith-based folks are excellent at sowing seeds.

You cannot turn on Christian TV without being taught the power in sowing a seed.

The problem that comes in is that **they are not taught how to bring in the harvest from the seed that they planted**.

Every spring, the farmer plants the seed in the ground but then, they go back in the field in the fall to actually bring in the harvest.

Faith-based people go to the mailbox.

That's a complete and total waste of time and it's not harvesting your seed.

The one place you will not find a farmer during harvest time is on a cruise ship or on vacation.

They are in their fields bringing in the harvest.

They don't "pray" that God brings in their harvest.

They don't "decree" that God is going to bring in their harvest.

They don't have "vision boards" about their harvest being in the barn.

Visit a farmer in the fall during harvest time and you will see them on their combines, sometimes late into the night, bringing in that harvest.

But Gods people plant a seed and then do nothing but wait for that financial miracle to supernaturally show up in their mailbox.

I call it the "Mailbox Millionaire Mentality"

I want to be crystal clear with you on this point.

God doesn't have any money in heaven, and he's not going to send you a check in the mail.

God operates through dreams and opportunities.

**God will give you a 6 or 7 figure dream, NOT a 6 or 7 figure check, and for most reading this book, he already has.**

I want to give you an example of this.

In my book publishing business, we have created over 100+ bestselling authors.

I have lived vicariously through the success of my clients.

When their books are successful, I get just as excited as if I wrote the book myself.

After I wrote my first book, "God Says When" which beat Joel Osteen and TD Jakes on the bestseller list for a day or two, I have been threatening to write a business book.

"God Says When" is a faith-based book that tells the story of my sudden cardiac arrest where I was clinically dead for 1.5 to 2

minutes, but it is NOT a business book.

So, for a couple of years now, I have been talking about releasing an actual business book.

One day, my wife Vickie came into my office and out of nowhere blurted," You really need to write that business book"

It shocked me.

We hadn't been discussing it and BAMM she hits me with that out of the blue.

But here is the thing.

It resonated with my spirit.

Hard.

I mean it hit me like a ton of bricks.

I just knew it was something that I was to do.

So that night, I came up with the title of the book, " Supernatural Success...Spiritual Laws I Used To Generate Over A Million Dollars In Sales And Beat Oprah In Website Traffic"

Then, I had my graphics department put together a cover for the book.

This happened within 24 hours.

I then posted the cover of the book on Facebook, Twitter and Linkedin announcing that my long-awaited business book was being released in 45 days.

The response was overwhelming.

People LOVED the title and cover and wanted to know how to get notifications indicating when it was going to be released, so they could buy a copy of the book.

I immediately began thinking to myself, I better write this book!

So I got busy and began writing the book and actually got it completed on time, and on the 45th day of the day that I said I will be publishing the book, I sat at my computer with the book ready to publish on Amazon, all I had to do was push one button and it would be published, and then it happened.

At that precise moment, this little fat man jumped up on my shoulder and began whispering in my ear.

Who do you think you are?

Do you really want to publish this book?

What if people don't like it?

You are writing a book on Supernatural Success, what if there is no Supernatural Success with this book?

The little fat man had some very valid points.

I knew that the book would debut on the bestseller list because that is the outcome that I deliver for my clients, but what if people read it and don't like it and worse yet, don't see "Supernatural Success" in their life.

I was plagued with self-doubt in that precise moment in time.

With all these valid points, the reality is like Ralph Kramden from the "Honeymooners", I had a BIG mouth and told EVERYONE when this book was going to be published on my social media accounts.

I had purposely boxed myself in when I had to publish the book at that moment, for no other reason than to honor my word and agreements.

So, I hit the publish button.

45 days after I published "Supernatural Success" Spiritual Laws I Used To Generate Over a Million Dollars in Website Traffic And Beat Oprah In Website Traffic", I signed a major TV deal based on the book that aired on 5 TV Networks including the WORD Network which is seen in over 200 Nations.

I also began to receive testimonies from people, there is the businessman who added 300k CASH money into his business account within 45 days of reading that book, and the businesswoman who only read the first 3 chapters and deposited 10k CASH into her account...so there's that.

One business Leader bought 50 copies to give to her leaders.

One woman bought 5 copies to give out as gifts.

So that little fat man was 100% wrong.

But I am not the only one that he has messed with.

**That little fat man stays busy, especially with those of you that have God-Given dreams.**

Even now with the release of this book, he has been busy.

What if this book is not as good as "Supernatural Success?"

Why risk it?

You can never top "Supernatural Success", why try?

So, for the little fat man, it seems he will always do his best to talk me out of my gift and I am certain he does the same thing with you.

But I am committed, and I know what my gifts are and the God-given dream that I have been given, so he can keep stepping.

But, are you starting to understand how all of this works?

God will give you a 6 or 7 figure dream, not a 6 or 7 figure check.

God gave me the idea for "Supernatural Success" and because I took the action, look at everything that was on the other side of that fear.

**Stop looking to God for money and start looking to God for that 6 and 7 figure dream or idea.**

That is where your prosperity is.

And for heavens sakes, tell that little fat man to SHUT UP!

This is YOUR moment in time.

This is YOUR Destiny.

This is YOUR God-Given dream.

You are not going to allow a little fat man to stop you.

Not you.

Not now.

Not ever.

# WHATEVER IT TAKES!

When I first wrote my best-selling real estate investing program, Vickie and I felt it was important to leave the people who bought that program with some encouraging words.

We choose a little missive called, "Whatever it Takes."

No one knows who wrote these words, but I heard that they were written by a Christian missionary who was about to be martyred for the cause of Christ in the morning and he wrote the following words the night before and placed them in his shoe.

It made a HUGE impact on the students who purchased the program.

We even had a testimonial, still on file, from a Pastor who was considering committing suicide until he bought our program and read Whatever it Takes!

We have also included it in our "God Says When" book and our "Supernatural Success" book.

If you read a book that I have written, you know it's going to have "Whatever It Takes" in it.

May it bless you the way it has countless people all around the world!

# WHATEVER IT TAKES

I am committed to doing "Whatever It Takes." I have the Power of the Holy Spirit. The die has been cast. I've stepped over the line. I am out of my comfort zone. The decision has been made. I'm a disciple of His. I won't look back, let up, slow down or back out. My past is redeemed, my present makes sense and my future is secure. I am finished and done with low living, sight walking, small planning, smooth knees, colorless dreams, tame visions, mundane talking, tiny giving, and dwarfed goals. I no longer need preeminence, prosperity, position, promotions or popularity. I don't have to be right. I don't have to be first, tops, recognized, praised, regarded or rewarded. I now learn by faith, love by patience, lift by prayer, and labor by power. My face is set, my gait is fast, my goal is heaven, my road is narrow, my way is rough, my companions few, my God reliable and my mission clear. I cannot be bought, compromised, detoured, lured away, turned back, diluted or delayed. I will not flinch in the face of sacrifice, hesitate in the presence of adversity, negotiate at the table of the enemy, ponder at the pool of popularity, or meander in the maze of mediocrity. I won't give up, shut up or burn up-till I've preached up, prayed up, paid up, stored up, and stayed up for the cause of Jesus Christ. I am a disciple of Jesus. I must go 'til I drop, preach 'til all know, and work 'til He stops. I'm going to hang on, hunker down, hug tight, and go where He wants me to go and let Him take me there. And when He comes to get His own, He'll have no trouble recognizing me because I have committed my life to doing...

WHATEVER IT TAKES!

# PLANT A SEED!

One of the spiritual laws that I have learned in my life is that whatever you help make happen in someone else's life, God will help make happen for you and your life.

If you need a miracle in your own life, then there is no faster way to your miracle than to help someone else who needs a miracle.

You will reap what you sow, no questions asked.

You now have the opportunity to share the "God Made Millionaire" message with so many who desperately need to hear this message, and by doing so, plant the seeds of harvest in your own life.

So many people are hurting today, in every area, marriage, health, family, and finances.

They feel like giving up and feel that there is no hope.

**Right now, you could probably think of 5-10 people who need to hear the message contained in this book.**

It is so easy to do.

Simply share the website to this book with them.

GodMadeMillionaire.com

Share it on Facebook, Twitter, and other social media platforms.

**Take a picture with you and this book and share it on your social media accounts and tag me in the post!**

Each time you do so, you are planting a miracle seed in someone else's life.

That to me is quite exciting.

If you bought the book on Amazon.com, please make sure that you leave a review.

It would be pretty cool if your review was the catalyst for someone to order the book and change their life... all because they read your review and the seed that you planted by leaving the review.

If you are involved in an MLM or network marketing business, if you really want to grow your business, plant a seed in your team by giving everyone that joins your business a copy of this book.

If I were in that business model, that's exactly one of the things I would do.

Scott Colley, of RedVikingTrucker.com, my good friend, once told me, "TC, I do not want to be involved in any business that does not have the breath of God on it."

I have always remembered that.

I believe God's breath is on this book.

**What you help make happen in someone else's life, God will help make happen in your life.**

You can be a conduit to someone's miracle just by sharing the link to this book, or even better, giving them a copy of this book.

I believe that you are here by divine appointment and for a reason.

It really is never too late for God to do a miracle in your life.

Never.

TC Bradley

"May the Lord bless you and keep you: May the Lord make His face shine upon you and be gracious unto you: May the Lord lift up his countenance upon you and give you peace."

# ABOUT THE AUTHOR

TC Bradley Is Undoubtedly A "Leader Amongst Leaders"

TC Is Known Worldwide For His Innovative Success And Business Strategies, Best-Selling Books, And RESULTS That He Helps His Clients Produce.

TC Provides Business and Success Consulting And Coaching To Those Exceptional Entrepreneurs Who Wish To Build An Empire.

TC Bradley has been seen on: The WORD Network, The Impact Network, Cornerstone Network, TCT Network, FOX4, 1 on One with Damon Davis, WINK-TV CBS, and high-powered digital publications, INC.com, USAToday.com, Small Business Trendsetters, and Business Innovators Magazine.

* Author of "God Says When" debuted #1 on the Amazon Best Seller list beating out such notable leaders like Joel Osteen and TD Jakes. (even if it was only for a day or two) we are proud of that accomplishment.

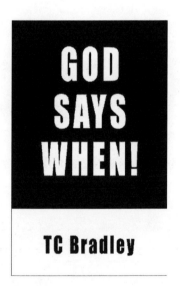

* Author of "Supernatural Success: Spiritual Laws I Used To Generate Over a Million Dollars In Sales And Beat Oprah In Website Traffic" debuted#1 on the Amazon Best Seller List and has been

featured on 4 Television Networks including The Word Network, The Impact Network, Cornerstone Network, TCT Network, FOX4, and 1 on One with Damon Davis.

* Creator of "Buy With No Credit" real estate investing program which sold over a million dollars of product from their first website that was launched in 2003, and within 2 years, had more traffic going to their website than Oprah had to go to her website.

* Founder of Instant Celebrity Status ® a global publishing and media firm for the exceptional entrepreneur!

"Who Wants To Be Seen On TV And Become A Best-Selling Author?"—100% Guaranteed.

www.InstantCelebrityStatus.com

\* Founder of God Made Millionaire ® a global community and brand for faith-based entrepreneurs!

Website: GodMadeMillionaire.com

For all media and speaking inquiries for TC Bradley, please contact our corporate headquarters at 1-800-676-1075 Ext.200

# LET'S GET SOCIAL!

Facebook.com/TCBradleyOfficial

Twitter.com/TCBradley

Instagram.com/godmademillionaires/

Made in the USA
Columbia, SC
29 July 2019